1/25

While I have attempted to standardise the recipes, they have not been tried
and tested. Mainly due to cost and waistline!

Jane Alliker

An Ebury Press book
Published by Random House Australia Pty Ltd
Level 3, 100 Pacific Highway, North Sydney NSW 2060
www.randomhouse.com.au

First published by Ebury Press in 2014

Cataloguing-in-Publication information available
from the National Library of Australia.

Cover and internal design by Amy Travers
Printed in China by Everbest Printing

Random House Australia uses papers that are natural, renewable and recyclable products
and made from wood grown in sustainable forests. The logging and manufacturing processes
are expected to conform to the environmental regulations of the country of origin.

The strength of this book is that the recipes and tips have been mostly provided by cancer patients — people from all walks of life and at various stages of their treatment.

I imagine that you have picked up this book because you or someone you love has embarked on life's hardest journey, the cancer journey.

My family and I were thrust into this journey when my beloved husband, Chris O'Brien, was diagnosed with a deadly brain tumour in November 2006. He passed away in June 2009.

Professor Chris O'Brien AO is the namesake of the Chris O'Brien Lifehouse — a new, state-of-the-art, comprehensive and integrated cancer centre situated on the Royal Prince Alfred Hospital and University of Sydney campuses.

He called his hospital Lifehouse because, as a surgeon and humanitarian, he knew that illness and death are a part of life itself, and this would be the House of Life, making the journey easier for those suffering from cancer.

Chris was a head and neck surgeon who experienced firsthand what the Americans were doing in the area of cancer care and treatment during his training in the United States in the 1980s. This started him on the path that would define the rest of his life.

During our time in the US, Chris saw dedicated facilities located across the country where patients were able to get everything they needed under one roof, in a facility that was also carrying out cancer research. These hospitals were called 'comprehensive cancer centres', and there were sixty across the country — and yet none in Australia.

I remember Chris saying at the time, 'If the Americans can do it, why can't we?'

Chris's dream to create a world-class centre of excellence for cancer treatment and education in Sydney developed from this experience, and he embraced a lifelong philosophy of patient care driven by research. As Head of Head and Neck Surgery at RPAH, he modelled his own department on these fundamental principles.

In 1998, Chris became a familiar face to many Australian households when he agreed to be part of a medical reality TV program called RPA. He was known as the compassionate and positive doctor who had such a kind and caring manner with his patients. He believed that every doctor should treat a patient as though they were a family member, and this is particularly important when dealing with cancer.

In 2003, Chris became the Director of the Sydney Cancer Centre based at RPAH. From this platform, he was able to transform the RPAH cancer program into a comprehensive cancer centre similar to those in the United States. In this one purpose-built facility, cancer patients could receive everything they needed, including complementary therapies, in a holistic environment that treated the entire person — body, mind and spirit. Their carers could also receive the critical support and education they would need during such a difficult time.

But importantly, he believed that the centre should be driven by medical research to give its patients the best chance of survival.

By 2006 the idea was gaining momentum with all the right people. However, just as Chris's vision was starting to take shape, the inspired leader faced a role reversal when he was diagnosed with an aggressive brain tumour. Over the years, Chris had helped thousands of cancer sufferers fight off their own sense of disempowerment, loneliness and fear, and now he was to travel the same path.

Chris met his diagnosis with selflessness, using it as a platform from which to gain even more momentum and draw attention to the need for a comprehensive cancer facility to be fully funded and supported by the broader community. In short, he turned his personal adversity into a national opportunity.

His vision is now a reality with the Chris O'Brien Lifehouse opening its doors to the public on November 19, 2013. Chris became an inspiration to the next generation of health professionals, and his spirit imbues every facet of the Chris O'Brien Lifehouse.

Chris and I walked the frightening path that many of you are now travelling. I, like you, scoured the internet for nutritional support for my precious husband, who was suffering the effects of chemotherapy, radiotherapy and surgery, and losing weight rapidly. Like you, we grasped at anything that would give us hope and did everything possible just so we could share another nanosecond together.

This collection of recipes and tips that Jane Alliker has painstakingly collected, and which have been so generously donated by patients and their carers, will help you on this journey. And I dearly hope that journey is made easier for you.

Chris's dream, passion, courage and determination have ensured that there will be something much better in the future for thousands of cancer patients. I wish to express my sincere gratitude to you for supporting the continued funding of the Chris O'Brien Lifehouse by buying this book.

I wish you confidence, hope and peace as you travel this road.

PROFESSOR CHRIS O'BRIEN AO

THE PATIENT CHEF

A collection of recipes and tips
donated by cancer patients, carers and chefs,
from the Chris O'Brien Lifehouse

EBURY
PRESS

contents

juices & smoothies

nix fix – good health juice

NICHOLAS DRAYSON
Lymphoma Non-Hodgkin's

On rising, squeeze ¼ lime or lemon in a large glass of warm water and drink it. Consume juice approximately half an hour later. This recipe is for one week's worth of juice (suggest you use juicer with a very large entry).

1 punnet alfalfa sprouts
2 bunches coriander leaves
1 bunch basil leaves
2 bunches parsley
10 medium carrots
1 white cabbage
1 red cabbage
12 beetroot, scrubbed
7 florets broccoli
1 whole cauliflower
2 knobs ginger
8 apples
1 bunch celery
2 white radishes
½ kg grapes
3 oranges

Juice the alfalfa, coriander, basil and parsley through the juice extractor followed by vegetable ingredients. Stir to combine. Refrigerate.

Optional additions

1 teaspoon Olive Leaf Extract

1/3 teaspoon Ultra Flora Plus probiotic (dairy free), contains 15 billion organisms

1 teaspoon Acai Berries Powder

Tablets: Garlic, Fish Oil, Spirilina, Vitamin C, Vitamin B12

Handful of Goji berries

sibby's good health remedy

SIBBY

Stomach Cancer

Sibby, my beautiful mum, had stomach cancer. She was giving up on living, sick as a dog and unable to look to a positive future. What did she do about it? She decided that her garden held her good health remedy. Herbal and veggie drinks became a regular addition to her diet and this together with the love and support from her family brought her back to good health and also gave her thirteen additional years to enjoy with her Grandies, Great Grandies and Great Great Grandies. Here are some of her juice formulas and advice. Half a cup at a time, taken between meals, is sufficient for good health.

for the blood

Equal parts of raw spinach or silver beet, celery, tomato and carrot juice.

A squeeze of lemon gives it extra zing, zap and zip.

for the nerves

Equal parts of grapefruit juice, celery and tomato.

The nerves seem to become a little bit rattled at times.

headache killer

(Makes 1 glass)

2/3 cup tomato juice

1/3 cup celery juice

1 teaspoon onion, finely chopped

other juice combos

Bunch of parsley, carrot, apple and cauliflower

Carrot, celery, parsley and broccoli

Pear, mint, orange and pineapple

the wonders of beetroot

Beetroot is very rich in iron, sodium, potassium and valuable fluorine. It should be eaten raw many times each week or juiced in several combinations with whatever is fresh in the garden. To some the taste is like rotten socks or mud. Just hold your nose and go for it. Here are some suggested juice combos:

Beetroot, carrot and pineapple

Beetroot, carrot and orange

Beetroot, celery, cucumber and apple

ian's special anti-nausea booster drink

MAGGIE MUNCASTER
Breast Cancer

A tasty, nutritious juice – the ginger eases nausea.

3 medium carrots
2 celery stalks
½ beetroot, scrubbed
1 small green apple
2 florets broccoli
½ cm ginger

Juice the carrots, celery, beetroot, apple, broccoli and ginger through a juice extractor. Stir to combine and serve.

Makes 1 large glass.

pola's 'wonder juice'

POLA CENCIGH
Hodgkin's Disease

3 medium carrots
2 celery stalks
1 large or 2 small green apples
1 beetroot, scrubbed
1 small piece of ginger

Juice the carrots, celery, apples, beetroot and ginger. Stir to combine and serve. Quantities can be adjusted to suit your personal taste. Store in the fridge and drink throughout the day.

Makes 1 large glass.

antioxidant juice

AVIVA'S RECIPE FOR WENDY

I gave this juice to Wendy every day for as long as I can remember, especially when she was going through chemo. She baulked some days but I sat there with her and we'd drink a massive glass together – room temperature is key as nutrients are absorbed almost immediately. The pomegranate juice is a new addition – it is one of the most powerful antioxidants we can consume. I have 125 ml every day for the heck of it. No harm in it.

1 large beetroot, scrubbed

2 medium carrots, unpeeled

1 cup fresh strawberries

4 cm piece fresh ginger, peeled – very important

1 cup watermelon (this helps sweeten)

1 large apple, unpeeled

handful blueberries or

125 ml fresh pomegranate juice

Juice all together through an extractor and drink at room temperature – not cold. Try to consume within 1 hour from start to finish.

Makes 1 litre.

tip

For nausea – ginger tea (ginger root and hot water) or ginger beer, toast, cheese and biscuits (plain water crackers or Jatz), homemade chicken soup with corn, plain rice and soy sauce and clean, fresh tart fruit like berries (nothing too sweet).

Susan Newell – Breast Cancer

veggie juice

MARGARET CARMICHAEL
Breast Cancer

6 medium carrots
½ bunch english spinach
2 celery stalks
1 medium cucumber
2 green apples
2 pears
2 large beetroot, scrubbed
3 cm fresh ginger
1 bunch parsley
¼ pineapple
2 tomatoes

Juice the carrots, spinach, celery, cucumber, apples, pears, beetroot, ginger, parsley, pineapple and tomatoes through a juice extractor. Stir to combine. Serve fresh. Enjoy!

Makes 1½ litres.

tip

For tiredness, I suggest short 'power' naps or Gastrolyte sachets. I also took Blackmores Travel Calm Ginger Tablets (about 2–3 at a time) between nausea medication. I also sipped on lemon juice with a spoonful of honey and a little warm water. Generally sipping is best for most beverages – such as gassy drinks or black or herbal tea (no milk).

Meredith Thirkettle – Rectal Cancer

white blood count juice

MARGARET CARMICHAEL
Breast Cancer

A friend of mine who went through chemo the year before me suggested this recipe to help keep my white blood cells up. I drank this juice every day and my blood count was good all through chemo. It also tastes quite nice.

1 apple, red or green
1 bunch alfalfa sprouts
1 medium carrot

Juice apple, alfalfa sprouts and carrot through a juice extractor. Stir to combine and serve.

Makes 1 small glass.

daily juice

CAMERON KIOSOGLOUS

5 organic apples
5 medium carrots
½ bunch celery
1 beetroot, scrubbed
green leaf (kale, spinach, chinese bok choy, broccoli leaf, cauliflower, etc)
1 lemon
1 lime
2 cloves garlic, peeled
ginger, to taste

Juice apples, carrots, celery, beetroot, green leaves, lemon, lime, garlic and ginger. Store in the fridge, stir to combine and drink throughout the day.

Makes 1 litre.

blueberry smoothie

SHARON SCOBLE
Breast Cancer

*I lived on these smoothies – they're yummo and immune-boosting to boot.
So I was always prepared, I cut bananas in half, peeled them and put them in
containers in the freezer ready for use. I also froze peaches or other seasonal
fruit.*

2 cups frozen blueberries or
mixed berries
1 cup vanilla soy milk
1 cup silken tofu
1 tablespoon honey
1 tablespoon ground flaxseed
¼ teaspoon lemon zest, optional
½ frozen banana

Blend blueberries, vanilla soy milk, tofu, honey, flaxseed, lemon zest and frozen banana in a blender until smooth.

Variations: you can substitute the soy milk and tofu for yoghurt and milk or juice.

Makes 1½ litres.

green smoothie

CAMERON KIOSOGLOUS

3 medium carrots
2 celery stalks
1 large or 2 small green apples
1 beetroot, scrubbed
1 small piece of ginger

Blend the carrots, celery, apples, beetroot and ginger in a blender until smooth. Store in the fridge and drink throughout the day.

Makes 1 litre.

basic smoothie

CAMERON KIOSOGLOUS

2 dates, pitted
1 banana
1 avocado
2 cups mixed nuts
(raw almonds, pine nuts,
pumpkin seeds, walnuts, etc)
1 cup berries
2 tablespoons chia seeds
1 tablespoon goji berries
1–2 teaspoons maca powder

Blend all ingredients in a blender until smooth and thick. Add a little water to thin if needed. Store in the fridge and drink throughout the day.

Makes 1 litre.

JUICES & SMOOTHIES

other juicing suggestions

SANDRA PELSEY

Carrot, apple and ginger juice.
Goes down well.

DIANNE MALLEN
Lung Cancer

Carrot, apple and celery juice.

One large glass each day.

JAMES JOHNSTON
Testicular Cancer

Whole carrot juice – 1 kg carrots (skin on)
through a juicer.

Watermelon and yoghurt.

Filtered water – 1 litre per day.

GAREFALIA MYLONAS
Eyes/Bones

Raw fruit and vegetavbles.

Cranberry juice.

JACK SWIEGERAS
Testicular Cancer

Apples – 10 a day and juiced.

STEWART AITKEN
Throat Cancer

Smoothies with yoghurt and ice cream.

Tip: be positive from Day 1, despite diagnosis.
Keep your sense of humour.

RUTH MILONAS
Lung Cancer

Fresh raw juices:
Carrot, celery, ginger and apple.
Cabbage, cucumber, tomato, onion and lettuce.

2–3 glasses per day.

salads & snacks

chris's lunchtime salad

CHRIS O'BRIEN

Brain Cancer

During the course of Chris's illness, I tried to find a balance between what I thought he should be eating and what he liked. The two sometimes were not compatible! Chris had a very sweet tooth but my reading about cancer taught me that tumour cells love sugar so I would endeavour to find a natural alternative. The following is roughly the routine we would follow.

I would incorporate foods that had a beneficial effect on retarding tumour growth as much as I could, but often it would come down to what Chris preferred to eat.

Gail O'Brien

100 g baby spinach leaves

2 tomatoes, chopped

2 beetroot, boiled or
roasted in foil

2 carrots, grated

200 g smoked trout or
salmon, flaked

sprinkle of mung beans and
chopped chives

dressing

3 tablespoons olive oil

2 tablespoons apple cider vinegar

1 teaspoon wholegrain mustard

1 teaspoon turmeric powder

Place all dressing ingredients into a jar, shake and set aside. In a large bowl combine spinach leaves, tomatoes, beetroot, carrots and flaked fish. Mix thoroughly. Arrange on serving plates, garnish with mung beans and chopped chives. Drizzle dressing over salad and serve.

Serves 1.

snack ideas

Raw vegetables (carrot, broccoli, celery and cauliflower) with hummus dip.

A handful of almonds.

A bowl of colourful fruit, especially melons, papaya, watermelon and blueberries.

chris's favourite lunch

CHRIS O'BRIEN
Brain Cancer

¼ cup low fat cottage cheese
or ricotta
1 tablespoon flaxseed oil
½ cup basil and chives, chopped
pinch turmeric powder
1 tomato, diced or sliced
2 tablespoons parsley, chopped
extra flaxseed or olive oil
2 slices non-wheat bread

(A modified version of the Dr Johanna Budwig Diet and Healing Protocol.)

In a bowl, combine the cottage cheese or ricotta and flaxseed oil; add the chopped basil, chives and pinch of turmeric. In a separate bowl combine tomato and parsley with oil. Toast your non-wheat bread and place onto your serving dish. Build your salad by spreading your toast with your cheese mixture topped with the tomato mixture.

Highly nutritious and medicinal!

Serves 1.

chickpea patties

CYNTHIA WORDEN
Breast Cancer and later Liver Cancer

For Cynthia Worden, who liked these when she came to visit me in Sydney.

3 x 300 g tins organic chickpeas
2 zucchini, grated
1 ½ cups breadcrumbs
¼ cup coriander, chopped
3 cloves garlic
2 teaspoons ground cumin
¼ teaspoon cayenne pepper
1 egg, beaten
salt and pepper, to taste
3 tablespoons olive oil, for frying

Drain the chickpeas. Place all the ingredients in a food processor and pulse until smooth. Divide into approximately 10 portions, depending on size, and shape into patties. Heat olive oil to medium in a non-stick frying pan and fry patties for 3–4 minutes on each side. Delicious served in a burger bun with avocado guacamole and side salad.

Note: the patties can be dipped in beaten egg and breadcrumbs before frying, but this is not necessary.

These patties freeze well.

Serves 4.

baked cheese pudding

GEORGINA

For Georgina, who loved this dish.

6 eggs

3 tablespoons milk and a little water

2 rashers bacon, chopped

100 g cheddar cheese, grated

1 tablespoon parmesan cheese, grated

salt and pepper, to taste

Preheat oven to 180°C. Grease an ovenproof dish. Beat the eggs and milk together then add bacon, cheeses and season with salt and pepper. Pour mixture into ovenproof dish. Bake for 45 minutes or until golden brown. Great served hot with salad or jacket potatoes, or can be served cold.

Variations: you can add whatever you like to the egg and milk mixture – mushrooms and peppers are good. You can also substitute the parmesan with feta.

Serves 2.

tip

As I couldn't drink tea or coffee, I instead used hospital grade Sustagen (chocolate) with full fat milk and ice cream to make a great chocolate milk shake.

I couldn't tolerate much at all, except spicy food and sugarless chewing gum with strong flavours.

David Brown – Head and Neck Cancer

SALADS & SNACKS

avocado salad

JOANNE KOJIC
Breast Cancer

cos lettuce, torn into pieces

1 avocado, sliced

1 mango, sliced

½ cup parmesan, shaved

2 tablespoons olive oil

2 tablespoons lemon juice

salt and black pepper,
to taste

mint, chopped, to serve

In your serving bowl combine lettuce, avocado, mango (drizzle juice from the cutting board over the salad when adding the mango) and parmesan cheese. In a separate bowl, whisk together olive oil, lemon juice, salt and pepper. Drizzle over salad. Sprinkle with chopped mint and serve.

Serves 2.

hummus

CHRIS O'BRIEN
Brain Cancer

340 g chickpeas, soaked
pinch sea salt
4 cloves garlic
3–4 tablespoons lemon juice
6 tablespoons tahine
carrot, celery, cucumber,
red capsicum, to serve

Drain chickpeas and place them in a large heavy-based saucepan. Cover with salted water, place over high heat and bring to the boil. Turn down to a medium heat and let simmer until the chickpeas are very soft. Drain chickpeas and reserve the cooking water. Place the chickpeas and garlic in a food processor with a third of a cup of the cooking liquid and pulse until smooth. Add the lemon juice and tahine and mix in well. You may need a little more cooking liquid to achieve a smooth, creamy consistency. The dip will thicken as it cools. Taste the hummus and season to your liking with more salt, garlic or lemon juice, or tahine can be added if desired. Serve hummus with sticks of carrot, celery, cucumber and red capsicum.

Serves a crowd.

spicy potato cakes

NO NAME OR DIAGNOSIS GIVEN

I ate these often as I found they had a good hot and spicy taste, which I found I needed during chemo.

1 cup mashed potato
1 cup sweet potato mash
2 eggs
2 tablespoons curry paste
3 tablespoons self-raising flour
2 tablespoons baking powder
½ cup fresh coriander, chopped
flour, for dusting
1 tablespoon olive oil
1 tablespoon butter

Combine potato mashes and add one egg at a time. Add the curry paste, flour, baking powder and coriander and mix through. Divide the mixture in 8 portions and shape into patties. Roll the patties in a little flour. Place oil and butter in a frying pan and heat to medium temperature. Fry potato cakes until brown on both sides. Great served with a red bean and chickpea salad.

Serves 4.

tip

My husband cooked me bacon, eggs and tomato as he knew it was what I liked most. I must say it started the mouth juices flowing. After not eating for around two days after treatment it was the best meal. It kind of kick-started me into eating again, which I love.

I'm also a lover of ginger – chocolate-coated ginger, ginger beer, ginger tea or meals cooked with ginger – which also helped with nausea.

For constipation – 2 teaspoons psyllium husk mixed with a large glass of water or fruit juice. I also took Omega 3, milk thistle or dandelion daily multivitamin.

Julene Lee – no diagnosis given

soft-boiled eggs with pickled beetroot and carrot

KYLIE KWONG

The inspiration for this dish came from a trip I took to Paris, where I loved the simple dishes of grated carrot, grated beetroot, celeriac rémoulade and hard-boiled eggs that are often served for lunch in some of the more traditional Parisian bistros . . . Just a drizzle of extra virgin olive oil and red wine vinegar would bring the vegetables alive. I have had this dish on my restaurant menu now for several years, using organic and biodynamic vegetables, and it's a great example of how ordinary, everyday ingredients become extraordinary when they are grown and harvested naturally. I love the vivid colours of the carrot and beetroot together, and the runny egg yolk combines with the dressing to make a beautifully rich sauce. Store the leftover Sichuan pepper and salt in an airtight container and use it to pep up stir-fries, salads and braises – it adds just the right amount of warmth and saltiness with a light citrus note.

150 g beetroot (about 1 medium-sized beetroot)
2 teaspoons brown sugar
1 teaspoon salt flakes
1 tablespoon brown rice vinegar
150 g carrot (about 1 large carrot)
2 eggs
1 lemon, cut into wedges
sichuan pepper and salt
1 tablespoon sichuan peppercorns
3 tablespoons salt flakes

dressing
1 egg yolk
¼ teaspoon salt flakes
1 tablespoon brown sugar
1 tablespoon brown rice vinegar
1 teaspoon tamari
¼ cup (60 ml) extra virgin olive oil

Peel and grate beetroot and place in a bowl, sprinkle with sugar and salt and mix well with fingers. Marinate for 2 hours.

While the beetroot is marinating, make the Sichuan pepper and salt. Dry-roast the Sichuan peppercorns and salt flakes in a heavy-based pan or wok. When the peppercorns begin to 'pop' and become aromatic, immediately remove from the heat. Allow to cool, then grind to a powder using a pestle and mortar or spice grinder.

Add brown rice vinegar to the beetroot, mix well, then strain beetroot, reserving the juice. Peel and grate carrot and set aside.

Carefully add eggs to a small pan of boiling water and simmer for 5 minutes until soft-boiled. Remove immediately and refresh under cold water, then peel and set aside.

To make dressing, whisk egg yolk and salt together in a small bowl until light and fluffy. Add sugar and whisk until creamy, then add vinegar and tamari, whisking to combine. Slowly drizzle in olive oil, whisking at the same time, until dressing is consistency of runny custard.

Arrange beetroot in a loose pile on a serving platter and drizzle with the reserved beetroot juice. Place carrot in a loose pile beside beetroot. Carefully cut eggs in half and sit them on platter. Drizzle dressing over carrot, then garnish with lemon wedges and a pinch of Sichuan pepper and salt. Serve.

Serves 4 as part of a shared meal.

cracked wheat and rice salad

LOUISE BISHOP
Breast Cancer

1/3 cup burghul
1 ¼ cups white rice
½ cup wild rice
1 x 425 g tin baby corn, drained
4 green shallots, chopped

dressing
2 tablespoons light soy sauce
¼ teaspoon sesame oil
2 tablespoons honey
1/3 cup oil
1 clove garlic, crushed

Place burghul in bowl, cover with boiling water and allow to stand for 15 minutes. Rinse burghul, drain and pat dry with absorbent paper. In two separate saucepans, bring water to the boil then add white rice in one and wild rice in the other. Boil, uncovered, for approximately 10 minutes or until just tender. Drain, rinse under cold water and drain well again. Combine burghul, rice, corn and shallots in bowl. For the dressing, combine all ingredients in screw-top jar and shake well. Add dressing to the bowl and mix gently. Cover and refrigerate for 1 hour before serving.

Serves 6.

mushroom loaf

NO NAME GIVEN
Breast Cancer

1 tablespoon olive oil
1 medium onion, chopped
500 g mushrooms, sliced
400 g cheddar cheese, grated
1 cup fresh breadcrumbs (about 3 slices bread)
1 teaspoon promite, optional
salt and pepper, to taste
1 egg, beaten

Preheat oven to 180°C. Grease and line a 20 cm loaf tin. Heat the oil in a pan. Add the onion and cook for 2–3 minutes or until tender. Add the mushrooms and cook for several minutes. Next add the cheese, breadcrumbs, Promite and seasoning to taste. Mix thoroughly. Remove from the heat, add the egg and mix well. Lightly press the ingredients into the loaf tin, cover with double foil and cook for 30 minutes. Remove the foil and cook for another 15 minutes. You can test whether it is cooked with a knife or skewer in the same way you would for a cake. Slice and serve. Great served hot or can be eaten cold the next day.

Variation: I sometimes add roasted sweet potato or any other vegetables, such as zucchini and carrots, to the mixture.

Serves 4.

SALADS & SNACKS

nut snack or breakfast

NICHOLAS DRAYSON
Lymphoma Non-Hodgkin's

Eat simple but powerful whole and good foods such as lean grilled meat, free range and organic chicken and all deep sea fish. Salmon (not farmed). Include raw or lightly steamed vegetables, or fresh salad with red, yellow, orange and green capsicum, carrots, red onion, tomatoes, mixed lettuce and tons of garlic (soak in lemon to reduce the smell).

should all be raw and organic
150 g almonds
150 g walnuts
150 g pistachios
200 g sunflower seeds
200 g pepitas
100 g sesame seeds
100 g psyllium husks
50 g lecithin granules
50 g linseed, crushed
50 g chai powder seed
100 g each raisins/sultanas/ cranberries

Combine all the ingredients and store in a large jar in a cool place. To serve for breakfast, add a base of spelt flakes to your bowl then your nut mixture followed by fresh blueberries, strawberries or mango and use either Soy or Almond or Rice Milk, and Manuka Honey to sweeten.

Drink lots of herbal teas (organic).

Walk, Love, Live and Pray.

tip

Almonds (with skin on) for when you lose your sense of taste. Sustagen for extra vitamins, and Metamucil (high-fibre diet) for tiredness.

Betsy Nix – Ovarian Cancer

simple crunchy asian salad

LYN SWINBURNE (RETIRED CEO, BCNA)
Breast Cancer

This salad is always a winner! So simple and easy to prepare – the freshness of the flavours makes this a great summer salad.

1 cos lettuce, shredded
1 bunch spring onions, chopped
½ bunch coriander, chopped
50 g pine nuts, lightly toasted
50 g flaked almonds, lightly toasted
1 packet dr chang's fried noodles

dressing

½ cup white sugar
¼ cup white vinegar
¼ cup light olive oil
4 tablespoons soy sauce

Place dressing ingredients into a pot, bring to the boil and continue to boil for 1 minute, stirring to combine. Allow to cool. Put the lettuce, spring onions and coriander in a bowl. Just before serving the salad, toast the pine nuts and lightly toast the almonds and add to the bowl. Add Dr Chang's fried noodles, then toss all the ingredients together with the dressing and serve immediately. Yum!

Serves 4.

fruity spaghetti salad

LOUISE BISHOP
Breast Cancer

Being prone to nausea and tummy upset, during chemo I chose to avoid certain foods, such as fish, chicken, pork, eggs and rich creamy sauces. I was given the tip of drinking ginger beer to relieve indigestion – it must be Bundaberg Ginger Beer! I chose to eat fresh vegetables, fruit, rice and pasta.

1 small rockmelon
1 small pineapple
125 g thin spaghetti pasta
1 cup almonds

marinade
1 tablespoon grated lime rind
1/3 cup lime juice
2 teaspoons honey
1 tablespoon fresh ginger, grated
1 teaspoon sugar

Cut rockmelon and pineapple into 2 cm pieces, place in a bowl and set aside. In a jar combine all the marinade ingredients and mix well. Combine the fruit with the marinade and mix thoroughly, then cover and refrigerate for 1 hour. Meanwhile, add pasta to a large pot of boiling salted water, boil uncovered until al dente; drain, rinse under cold water, drain again. In a large serving bowl combine undrained fruit mixture, pasta and nuts. Mix well and serve.

Serves 4–6.

zucchini bake

DIANE
Lung Cancer

½ cup butter or oil
6 medium zucchini, sliced
2 cloves garlic, crushed
250 g mushrooms, sliced
1 x 800 g tin diced tomatoes
1 cup fresh brown breadcrumbs
(about 3 slices bread)
1 cup sour cream
1 teaspoon paprika
1 tablespoon almonds, chopped
salt and pepper, to taste
½ cup parmesan, grated

Preheat oven to 180°C. Heat half of the butter or oil in a frying pan. Add zucchini and cook until just tender. Using a slotted spoon, remove zucchini from pan and place in a bowl, set aside. Add the rest of the butter or oil, garlic and mushrooms to the pan and fry, stirring, for about 3–5 minutes until the mushrooms are cooked. Add the tomatoes and cook for a few minutes. Stir in the breadcrumbs, sour cream, paprika and almonds, mix well. Season with salt and pepper. Remove pan from the heat and stir through the zucchini. Pour the mixture into an ovenproof casserole dish, sprinkle with parmesan and bake for 30 minutes or until golden brown.

This dish tastes even better the second day!

Serves 4.

burghul salad

RPA PATIENT (NO NAME OR DIAGNOSIS GIVEN)

This salad is great to take with you on hospital visits.

100 g burghul wheat
1 medium onion, finely chopped
1 red capsicum, finely diced
1 green capsicum, finely diced
50 g lentils (tinned is fine)
50 g cashews or peanuts, lightly toasted
2 teaspoons dried mixed herbs, tarragon and chives
juice and grated rind of 1 lemon
sea salt and black pepper, to taste
lemon wedges for garnish

Place burghul wheat in a large mixing bowl and cover with boiling water. Set aside for 10 minutes until the water is absorbed and the wheat is soft. Add onion, capsicums, lentils, nuts, herbs, lemon juice and lemon rind to burghul wheat and mix together well. Season to taste. Garnish with wedges of lemon.

Serves 2.

oven baked apples served with rice

SANDY WATSON, PREPARED WITH LOVE FOR HER HUSBAND JOHN
Pancreatic Cancer

This recipe helps soothe feelings of nausea, especially after chemotherapy. Also helps to overcome reflux and indigestion if eaten slowly. And as John comments, 'It tastes better than it looks!'

4–6 small eating apples (gala, delicious, pink lady), cored

selection of dates, prunes, mixed dried fruit, to taste

Preheat oven to 160°C. Score your apples around the middle then roughly chop your choice of dates, prunes and mixed fruit and combine in a bowl. Stuff the cavity of your apples with mixed fruit. Place apples in an ovenproof dish large enough to accommodate them, then pour water into the dish until it comes part way (about a third) up the apples. Bake for up to 2 hours or until apples are very soft. Cover apples with foil or a lid part way through to prevent excess browning. Serve warm with rice (I use basmati as that's what I like), or on their own. The resulting cooking liquid is what makes this dish soft, moist and easy to digest, so make sure you spoon some of the delicious juices over the apples.

Apples keep in the fridge for up to 6 days.

Tip: while coring and scoring the apples, squeeze a little lemon juice inside the cavity to prevent them from browning.

Variation: add a little brown sugar or honey to the mixture in the cavity. You can also add a little cinnamon or nutmeg to the fruit mixture before stuffing.

Serves 2–4.

easy zucchini slice

NO NAME OR DIAGNOSIS GIVEN

2 zucchini, chopped
1 onion, chopped
½ cup strong cheddar cheese
½ cup milk
½ cup flour
3 eggs
¼ cup oil

Preheat oven to 200°C. Grease a shallow pie dish. Blend all ingredients together in a food processor. Place the mixture into your pie dish and cook for 20–30 minutes or until golden brown.

Great served hot or cold.

Serves 2.

turkish omelette

AHMAT DEPRELI
Hodgkin's Lymphoma

2–3 eggs
salt and pepper
½ cup cheese, grated
1 tablespoon butter
1 tablespoon olive oil
1 onion, chopped
1 capsicum, diced
4 thin slices turkish salami

Break the eggs into a bowl, season with salt and pepper and whisk together. Add cheese and mix through. Heat the butter and oil in a frying pan and sauté the onion and capsicum until softened. Add the salami and cook for 1 minute. Turn the heat to low and pour the egg mixture into the pan. Stir once or twice, then cover and cook slowly over low heat until set. Serve with Turkish bread.

Serves 1.

chilli tomato sauce

NO NAME GIVEN
Breast Cancer

1 tablespoon olive oil
1 onion, finely chopped
½ clove garlic, crushed
arge red chilli, seeds removed and
finely chopped
1 x 400 g tin diced tomatoes
heaped tablespoons tomato paste
salt and pepper, to taste

Heat the oil in a frying pan on medium heat, add onion and cook until soft. Add garlic and chilli and cook, stirring, for another minute. Stir in the tomatoes and tomato paste. Bring to the boil then simmer for 5 minutes until the sauce thickens a little. Season with salt and pepper to taste. This is an easy sauce that can be used with pasta, rice or couscous.

Variation: for more nutrition, even if you can't taste them, chop up some mushrooms and add to the sauce.

Makes ½ litre.

tip

Lemon and/or lime squeezy with soda water for when you know you should have more fluid but the taste in your mouth puts you off.

Michelle Smith – Fallopian Tube Cancer

soups with substance

patsy's pumpkin soup

GWEN JOYNES
Peritoneal Cancer

Try to keep as active as possible and get out with friends – if you are feeling lousy it does help, and talking and interacting with friends and family helps to take your mind off some troubles. Keep cheerful, and if asked 'How do you feel?' say good, or okay, and you will feel okay. If you are very sick, talk to your oncologist – there is help available.

2 tablespoons butter
1 tablespoon curry powder
1 large onion, finely chopped
3 chicken cubes or
chicken stock powder
2½ cups water
1 pumpkin, peeled and cubed
2 large potatoes, peeled and cubed
chilli, optional

Melt butter in a saucepan. Add curry powder and onion and cook until onion is soft. Meanwhile add chicken cubes or stock powder to water, mix well and pour over onion. Bring to the boil. Add pumpkin and potato (also add the chilli now if desired) and cook until tender. When cooled, process in a blender in batches until smooth. Reheat before serving if necessary.

Note: to make cutting up the pumpkin easier, place the whole pumpkin in microwave oven for approximately 5 minutes. Cut into cubes before removing skin – easy.

Less curry powder may be used according to taste. Freezes well.

Serves 4.

carrot and ginger soup

DIANE IRVING
Breast Cancer

While preparing this soup, I pass the time by thinking of everything that has to be grown to go in it. I live on a farm at Rollands Plain on the Mid North Coast of New South Wales and appreciate freshly grown vegetables, and these simple thoughts set me daydreaming. Of course, I have a glass of red wine of an evening with soup and fresh bread! This soup tastes great, is ready to eat in 25 minutes, and freezes well too.

3 cups vegetable stock
1 tablespoon oil
1 onion, diced
1 tablespoon freshly grated ginger
1 kg carrots, roughly chopped
2 tablespoons fresh coriander, chopped
salt and pepper, to taste

Place the stock in a large saucepan and bring to the boil. In a separate large heavy-based pan, heat the oil, add the onion and ginger and cook for 2 minutes, or until the onion has softened. Add the carrots to the stock and bring to the boil, then reduce the heat and simmer for 10–15 minutes, or until the carrots are soft and tender. Allow to cool slightly, place in a blender or food processor and process in batches until smooth. Return to the pan and add a little more stock or water to thin the soup to your desired consistency. Stir through the coriander and season to taste. Heat gently before serving.

Serves 4.

pear and apple soup

RPA PATIENT (NO NAME OR DIAGNOSIS GIVEN)

*A delicious soup that takes away the metallic taste and gives me the goodness
I need.*

2 tablespoons oil
1 large onion, diced
2 medium carrots, chopped
2 tablespoons sugar
2 tablespoons mild curry powder
½ teaspoon cumin powder
½ teaspoon salt
2 pears, peeled and chopped
2 granny smith apples, peeled and chopped
2 cups vegetable stock
2 cups water

Heat oil in a large heavy-based saucepan. Add onion and carrots and sprinkle with sugar. Cook for 8–10 minutes, stirring often, until the onion and carrots are caramelised. Add curry powder, cumin and salt and cook for 30 seconds. Add pears and apples and mix well, then add stock and water. Simmer on low for 15 minutes. Allow to cool slightly, then pour into a blender in batches and puree until smooth. Can be served warm with almond meal on top, or cold with yoghurt.

Serves 4.

pumpkin and ginger soup

NO NAME OR DIAGNOSIS GIVEN

This soup is filling and easy to prepare. Keeps well in the fridge for a few days and freezes well.

½ butternut pumpkin
1 large sweet potato
6–7 potatoes
2 tablespoons olive oil
2 teaspoons cumin
salt and pepper, to taste
4–5 cups boiling water
grated ginger, to taste
coriander, chopped, to serve

Peel pumpkin, sweet potato and potatoes and roughly chop. In a large heavy-based saucepan, heat the olive oil. Add vegetables and cumin to the pan and season with salt and pepper to taste. Place lid on the pan and cook for 5 minutes, stirring occasionally. Next add enough boiling water to cover the vegetables and simmer until soft. Set aside to cool slightly then transfer to a blender and process until smooth. Add more cumin if required, or some ginger to taste. To serve sprinkle with a little freshly chopped coriander.

Serves 4–6.

tip

Rinse mouth with a sodium bicarbonate mouthwash – 1 teaspoon of sodium bicarbonate to 1 cup of lukewarm water – before and after meals to help with taste.

Ei-Kazzi – Breast Cancer

beetroot soup

FELICIYA LEIMONTAILE
Breast Cancer

This soup is good for the blood and for the liver.

olive oil
1 large onion, diced
1 clove garlic, minced
2–3 fresh beetroot, peeled and diced
1 cup carrots, diced
2 cups cabbage, shredded
3 potatoes, peeled and cubed
4 cups vegetable or beef stock
3–4 cups water
salt and pepper, to taste
1 tablespoon lemon juice
1 tablespoon sour cream, to serve

Heat olive oil in a large stock pot over medium heat. Sauté onion and garlic, and cook until softened. Add the beets, carrots, cabbage and potatoes and sauté for about 5 minutes. Cover the vegetable mix with the stock and water, place the lid on and simmer until cooked. If puréeing, let the soup cool a little before processing in the blender. Season with salt and pepper to taste and add lemon juice. Serve soup garnished with sour cream.

Serves 4.

bean soup

NO NAME GIVEN
Gum Cancer

2 tablespoons olive oil
1 onion, diced
2 cloves garlic, minced
2 carrots, peeled and chopped
2 sticks celery, ends trimmed and chopped
1 litre vegetable stock
1 x 800 g tin tomatoes
1 x 420 g tin five bean mix or red kidney beans
herbs (optional)
spinach (optional)
sprinkling of parmesan to serve

Heat oil in a large heavy-based saucepan over medium heat. Add onion and gently cook, stirring, until softened. Add garlic and cook for 1 minute. Add carrots and celery and cook for a further 5 minutes, stirring occasionally. Add the stock and tomatoes and bring to the boil. Add the Five Bean mix and any herbs you like (or even some spinach) and cook until the vegetables are soft. Allow to cool slightly, before placing into a blender in batches and process on pulse. Return to the pan and warm through. Add a sprinkling of parmesan to serve.

Serves 4.

simple potato soup

DOMINI STUART
Breast Cancer

Soup is wonderful for eating in small quantities throughout the day when your appetite is a little jaded. Simple Potato Soup was the only thing I could face after my first chemotherapy treatment but, if you don't feel nauseous, go straight past this recipe. Bland isn't the word! Tasty Potato Soup (on the next page) is the basis for any number of delicious vegetable soups – simply replace one or more potato with a similar weight of carrots, parsnips, sweet potato, leeks, cauliflower, broccoli or anything else you fancy.

1 onion, finely chopped

a tiny amount of oil

4 large potatoes, peeled and roughly chopped

a little salt if you like it

In a large heavy-based saucepan, sauté the onion slowly in the smallest possible quantity of oil, or oil with a little water, until it's transparent. Add the potatoes, enough water to barely cover them and salt if you're using it. Bring to the boil and simmer until the potatoes are very tender. Set aside to cool, then purée the soup in a blender or food processor.

Serves 2–4.

tasty potato soup

DOMINI STUART
Breast Cancer

1 tablespoon vegetable oil
1 onion, chopped
3–4 cloves garlic, chopped
4 large potatoes (or equivalent),
roughly chopped
500 ml water
2 teaspoons vegemite or promite,
or 2 vegetable stock cubes
herbs – preferably fresh, such as
parsley, oregano, sage or thyme
500 ml milk or soy milk

In a large saucepan, heat the oil and gently sauté the onion and garlic until soft. Add the chopped vegetables and stir well. Add the water, Vegemite or Promite, or stock cubes and herbs. Simmer for about 30 minutes or until the vegetables are very soft. Remove from the heat, allow to cool and purée in a food processor or blender until smooth. Return to the pan and stir in the milk or soy milk and reheat without boiling.

Variation: to make the soup even tastier still, throw in a few spices just before you add the vegetables and water, and stir over a low heat for a minute: $\frac{1}{2}$ – 1 teaspoon each of ground cumin, coriander and cardamom are good to start with. If your mouth isn't too sore, add a teaspoon of ginger and a pinch of chilli powder.

Serves 4.

vegetable soup with chickpeas

ANNIE CAMPBELL FOR LUCI
No diagnosis given

These are some recipes that Luci was able to enjoy while she was on chemo, although she could only have small amounts at a time. Luci could also eat fresh strawberries and cherries and found drinking Ribena with ice and water quite palatable.

for the chickpeas

250 g fresh raw chickpeas

1 celery stalk, finely chopped

4 cloves garlic, crushed

small bunch thyme sprigs

2 bay leaves

tablespoon extra virgin olive oil

for the soup

2 carrots, finely chopped

1 onion, finely chopped

1 red onion, finely chopped

2 celery stalks, finely chopped

cob corn, kernels taken off cob

1 tin chopped tomatoes or 2 tomatoes, finely chopped

thyme leaves

salt and pepper, to taste

1 litre chicken stock

Soak the chickpeas in at least double their volume of cold water and leave overnight. Drain the chickpeas and put them in a large pan with the celery and garlic. Add the herbs tied together, the olive oil and double the quantity of water as that of the chickpeas. Cover and bring to the boil, then turn down the heat and simmer for about 1½ hours, adding more water if necessary. Take off the heat and keep to one side.

Heat a little more olive oil in a pan and add the carrots, onions, celery and corn and cook gently until soft. Add the tomatoes, thyme leaves and season with salt and pepper to taste. Then add the chicken stock and cook for 20 minutes or until vegetables are soft and soup has good flavour. Drain the chickpeas and add in the last 5 minutes of cooking to heat through. Serve.

Any vegetables can be used and the chickpeas can be left out if desired. The soup can also be put into a food processor and blitzed until smooth.

Serves 4–6.

kylie's hearty vegetable soup

KYLIE KWONG

I have always drooled over the rustic, peasant-style soups of Italy. For me, they reflect the earthiness and generosity of Italian home cooks – it's as if the cook goes into their thriving backyard vegetable patch, picks anything and everything, then just throws it all into the same pot. The addition of the pork bones gives this soup a lovely smoky flavour but of course is not essential. For a vegetarian version, simply omit the pork bones and use a vegetable stock instead of a chicken one. I just love all the different textures, flavours, shapes, sizes and colours of the vegetables, and the final grating of parmesan cheese, which slowly melts through the soup, sends me into orbit.

chicken stock

1.5 kg chicken or chicken bones and wings

4 litres cold water

10 spring onions, trimmed and cut in half crossways

1 large red onion

7 cm piece ginger, sliced

10 cloves garlic, crushed

3 tablespoons extra virgin olive oil

65 g smoked pork belly or bones

4 cloves garlic, crushed

1 white onion, sliced

2 teaspoons salt flakes

3 sprigs thyme

2 sticks celery, sliced

4 baby carrots, peeled, cut in half lengthways

1 small fennel bulb, sliced

1 potato, roughly diced

3 ripe tomatoes, roughly diced

2 litres of chicken stock

280 g fresh green peas

1 zucchini (courgette), roughly diced

180 g cavolo nero, washed, stems removed, leaves sliced

First make the stock. If using a whole chicken, rinse it thoroughly and trim away excess fat from inside and outside the cavity. Place chicken or bones and wings in a large, heavy-based pan or stock pot, along with all the remaining stock ingredients. Bring to the boil, then reduce heat to a gentle simmer, skimming the surface with a ladle to remove any impurities. Turn down heat until the surface of the stock is barely moving and cook for 2 hours, skimming as required. Remove stock and discard chicken pieces. Strain stock through muslin.

Heat olive oil in a large, heavy-based pan or stock pot, then add pork, garlic, onion, salt and thyme and fry for 5 minutes. Add celery, carrots, fennel, potato and tomato and fry for 5 minutes. Add 2 litres of the chicken stock and bring to the boil. Simmer gently for 25 minutes. Add peas, zucchini and cavolo nero and simmer for a further 10 minutes.

Adjust seasoning, then serve with fresh parmesan and crusty bread.

Tip: Silver beet can be used as a substitute for cavolo nero.

Serves 4–6.

hearty congee

LINDA ISHIBASHI
Breast Cancer

1 cup cooked rice
½ onion, chopped
1 rasher bacon, chopped
1 ½ cups chicken stock
1 teaspoon garlic, minced
1 teaspoon ginger, minced
1 cup cabbage, shredded
salt and white pepper, to taste
½ cup bean sprouts
1 teaspoon soy sauce, to serve
1 hard-boiled egg, quartered, to serve

Put rice, onion, bacon and chicken stock in a stock pot and bring to boil. Add garlic, ginger and cabbage and keep stirring until rice is slightly thickened. Season with salt and pepper then add bean sprouts. Stir for 5 minutes then ladle into a bowl and serve with soy sauce and hard-boiled egg.

Serves 2–4.

tip

Sucking on frozen pineapple strips helps relieve the metallic taste in the mouth.

Joanne Kosic – no diagnosis given

moreish mains

fish with pine nut sauce

baked chicken breast

silvio's special fish dish

pan-fried reef fish with piperade, smoked eggplant purée and
olives

steamed fish with ginger and shallots

quick and easy fish

tarsha's tuna glug

lemon fish

hot ginger garlic fish

other dinner suggestions

beef casserole

chicken tagine

shepherd's pie

crumbed lamb's fry

the original cornish pastry

daube wagyu beef cheeks with baby carrots, leeks, button
mushrooms, paris mash and a red wine reduction

george's vegetable lasagne

simple fettuccine

macaroni cheese

meatless spaghetti bolognese

tortellini with mushroom sauce

penne all'arrabbiata

quick macaroni cheese

greek pasta

puttanesca sauce

baked chicken and pumpkin risotto

fish with pine nut sauce

NO NAME OR DIAGNOSIS GIVEN

1 kg any whole white fish
olive oil
salt and pepper, to taste
1 cup pine nuts
2–3 large cloves garlic
pinch salt
1 cup lemon juice
parsley, for garnish

Preheat oven to 200°C. Brush the fish all over with olive oil. Season with salt and pepper to taste. Wrap fish in foil, which is also oiled. Place in a baking pan and cook for 30 minutes. Grind pine nuts, garlic and salt. Gradually add lemon juice, stirring constantly, until it looks like yoghurt. Remove fish from oven. Transfer fish to a serving dish, cover with pine nut sauce and garnish with parsley.

Serves 4–6.

baked chicken breast

GRACE DUREAU
Breast Cancer

This dish is simple to make and easy to digest while having chemo.

2 chicken breast fillets, skin removed
1 tablespoon tamari organic soy sauce
2 teaspoons dry sherry
2 cloves garlic, minced
2 teaspoons freshly grated ginger
1 tablespoon mint, chopped
salt

Preheat oven to 180°C. Combine together soy sauce, sherry, garlic, ginger and mint then pour over chicken and set aside to marinate for 30 minutes. Place chicken in a small ovenproof baking dish, season with salt and sprinkle with spring onion. Bake in the oven until tender – check the chicken after 10 minutes. Pour pan juices over chicken and rice. Serve.

Serves 1.

silvio's special fish dish

SILVIO BRASIL
Hodgkin's Lymphoma

3 basa fillets
lemon salt
3 potatoes, thinly sliced
3 tomatoes, sliced
1 onion, thinly sliced
salt and pepper, to taste
small bunch coriander, finely
chopped
capers, to taste
1 tablespoon coconut cream
½ cup chicken stock

Preheat oven to 160°C. To prepare the fish, place the fillets in a dish, sprinkle both sides with lemon salt, cover and set aside for 30 minutes. In a 2 litre, 5 cm deep casserole dish, layer half of the potatoes, tomatoes and onion and season to taste. Sprinkle the coriander and capers over the vegetables and then top with the fish fillets. Layer the remaining vegetables on top of the fish. Combine coconut cream and stock together then pour over. Cook for 30–40 minutes or until the fish and vegetables are cooked through when tested with a fork. Serve with salad and rice.

Serves 3.

pan-fried reef fish with piperade, smoked eggplant purée and dried olives

MATT MORAN

300 g pitted black olives

6 x 200 g portions reef fish, skin on

1 head baby fennel, finely shaven with a vegetable peeler

olive oil, to serve

piperade

3 red capsicums

40 ml olive oil

½ spanish onion, sliced

1 clove garlic, chopped

6 anchovy fillets, chopped

6 tomatoes, seeded and chopped

100 ml sherry vinegar

1 tablespoon parsley, chopped

salt and pepper

smoked eggplant

2 eggplants

½ teaspoon ground cumin

2 tablespoons Greek yoghurt

method

Preheat the oven to 130°C

To prepare the olives, spread them flat on a baking tray then place them in the oven for approximately 3 hours until they become crumbly. Remove and allow to cool.

To prepare the piperade, place the capsicums over a high, naked flame or under a hot grill until the skin has been blackened all over then transfer them to a bowl. Cover the bowl tightly with plastic wrap and then set aside for 10–15 minutes. Once cooled, peel and deseed the capsicums then dice them into pieces approximately 1 cm in size.

Heat half of the olive oil in a saucepan and when hot add the Spanish onion. Cook over moderate heat for 2–3 minutes ensuring they do not gain colour. Add the garlic and anchovies then cook for a further 2 minutes. Add the diced capsicum and tomatoes then cook for a further 20–30 minutes until the tomato has broken down and the sauce has reduced to a thick consistency. Add the vinegar and chopped parsley then season with salt and pepper. Set aside until required.

Preheat a grill or BBQ.

To prepare the smoked eggplant, place the eggplants onto a hot grill or BBQ and cook for approximately 20 minutes, turning every 5 minutes until the eggplants are tender all the way through. Once cooked, remove the eggplants from the grill or BBQ, allow them to cool slightly then cut them in half and scoop out flesh. Roughly chop the flesh then stir in the cumin and yoghurt until combined. Set aside until required.

Preheat oven to 170°C

To prepare the fish, heat a little olive oil in an ovenproof fry pan over moderate heat and when hot place the fish fillets into the pan skin side down. Cook for 2 minutes or until golden and then transfer the fry pan to the oven. Bake for 4–5 minutes and then remove the pan from the oven. Turn the fish over and allow to cook for 1 minute using the residual heat in the pan. Remove the fish from the fry pan and place covered on a plate until required.

To serve, place some of the piperade and smoked eggplant on a plate and top with the fish. Garnish with fennel, black olives and drizzle with olive oil.

Serves 6.

MOREISH MAINS

steamed fish with ginger and shallots

CHRIS O'BRIEN
Brain Cancer

This is Chris's favourite fish dish.

1 snapper fillet
2 spring onions, finely sliced
1 cm piece ginger, chopped
2 tablespoons coriander, chopped
soy sauce, to taste
¼ cup olive oil

Place steamed fish on a plate and sprinkle with spring onions, chopped ginger and chopped coriander mixed together. Douse the fish with soy sauce until it is stained and there is a thin layer of soy sauce at the bottom of the plate. Heat the olive oil in a saucepan and carefully pour hot oil over the fish. Serve with steamed greens topped with oyster sauce sprinkled with fresh parsley and chives.

Serves 1.

quick and easy fish

TARSHA GALE
Breast Cancer

Tip: don't drink coffee on the day of chemo because you want your veins to be hydrated – drink lots of water in the lead-up.

200 g deep sea perch fillet
1 tablespoon soy sauce
juice of 1 lime
½ teaspoon minced ginger
chilli flakes, to taste

Preheat oven to 180°C. Lightly score the fish fillet. Combine the soy sauce, lime juice, ginger and chilli and cover the fish in the marinade. Transfer into an ovenproof baking pan, wrap fish in foil and bake for 15–20 minutes. Serve with steamed vegetables.

Easy, tasty and quick.

Serves 1.

tarsha's tuna glug

TARSHA GALE
Breast Cancer

2 cups boiled or steamed rice
500 g tinned tuna
1 x 400 g tin crushed pineapple
1 x 400 g tin corn kernels
1 onion, finely chopped
½ cup cheese, grated
salt and lemon pepper, to taste

Mix all ingredients together. Season with salt, pepper or lemon pepper. To serve, microwave each serve for 40 seconds – yum!

Keeps well in fridge/freezer for regular small serves.

Serves 2–4.

tip

During six months of chemotherapy, I dealt with the nausea effects by drinking ginger tea. Take one piece of ginger, peel it, cut into thin slices and put in thermos, and add hot water. Drink before and after, even during chemo! I found the anti-nausea drugs given along with first batch of chemo made me very nauseous!

Ros Lawson – Breast Cancer

lemon fish

JUNE ELLIOTT
Breast Cancer

I found cooking fish in citrus juices and large slices of garlic was tasty.

400 g white fish fillets
½ lime, sliced
½ lemon, sliced
2 cloves garlic, crushed
sea salt and pepper, to taste

Preheat oven to 180°C. Wrap fish in foil with slices of lime and lemon, sprinkle with crushed garlic, sea salt and ground pepper. Transfer to a baking pan and bake in oven for 20–30 minutes (depending on size of fish).

Serves 2.

hot ginger garlic fish

MARY THISWALL
Head and Neck Cancer

2 large fillets of fish
5 cm piece ginger, julienned
3 cloves garlic, julienned
1–2 small red chillies, sliced
¼ cup lime juice
½ bunch coriander, roughly chopped
salt and pepper, to taste

Preheat the oven to moderate 180°C. Line a baking tray with foil and lightly grease with oil. Place each fish on the foil and sprinkle over ginger, garlic and chillies. Pour lime juice onto fish, season with salt and pepper and wrap firmly in foil. Bake for 15–20 minutes, until the flesh flakes easily when tested with a fork. To serve, transfer to serving plate and garnish with coriander.

Serves 2.

other dinner suggestions

vegetarian stir-fry
: Lots of veggies with ginger, coriander and rosemary. Serve with rice noodles.

Christine Ritchie – Multiple Myelomas

chicken stir-fry
: Organic chicken stir-fried with olive oil and lots of vegetables, served with brown rice.

Valerie Cummings – Lung Cancer

tip

I wasn't enjoying food at all until a friend baked a beautiful roast dinner for me. It seemed to bring my taste buds back! I recommend full baked roast chicken and vegetable dinners. Crockpot cooking keeps all the goodness in, and leftovers can be blended to a soup the next day. I avoided processed foods (white foods), and ate fruit – particularly blueberries and bananas – for tiredness.

Sarah Corruthers – Breast Cancer

beef casserole

FORTUNATA MONTEVERDI
Ovarian Cancer

2 carrots, peeled and cubed
handful green beans, trimmed
and cut into 3 cm pieces
3 potatoes, peeled and cubed
small head of broccoli, cut into
florets
¼ cauliflower, cut into florets
500 g beef steak, trimmed of
fat and cut into cubes
packet of french onion soup

Preheat the oven to 200°C. Place all the vegetables and beef in a 2 litre x 5 cm baking dish. Sprinkle with French onion soup. Pour over 2 cups of water. Cover with lid or foil and cook for 20 minutes. Cook uncovered for a further 15 minutes or until the meat and vegetables are cooked and brown. Transfer straight to the table and serve with crusty bread.

Serves 2.

tip

Percy Weston's Australian-made supplement, Percy's Powder. A 1.4 g sachet of Percy's Powder stirred into a glass of water with the juice of half a lemon makes a refreshing effervescent drink. Percy's Powder is a blood tonic and may help maintain normal blood. The mineral salts in Percy's Powder readily dissolve in water or fruit juice to supply the body with a means of checking the build-up of acids and phosphates. Percy's Powder helps to flush out the acids (acid build-up in the tissues can cause infection and chronic fatigue).

Frederick Phan – Soft Tissue Sarcoma

chicken tagine

ROZ
Breast Cancer

1 kg chicken merrylands or thighs

2 tomatoes, 1 chopped, 1 sliced

2 onions, 1 chopped, 1 sliced

2 large potatoes, cut into wedges

150 g green olives, pitted

1 bunch coriander, chopped

1 cup water

1 preserved lemon, rind only, cut into wedges

chermoula marinade

2 cloves garlic

½ preserved lemon

2 onions

½ chilli

1 tablespoon sweet paprika

1 tablespoon ground cumin

2 tablespoons coriander

2 tablespoons parsley

2 bay leaves

½ teaspoon saffron strands soaked in 2 tablespoons water

½ cup olive oil

salt, to taste

Day 1. Chermoula: combine the marinade ingredients in a food processor and blend until finely chopped and thoroughly combined. Leave to stand for 30 minutes before using (this can be made up to 7 days in advance and stored in the refrigerator). In a large bowl mix your chicken pieces with half the chermoula marinade and refrigerate for at least 2 hours or ideally overnight.

Day 2. In your tagine or heavy-based dish, combine the chopped tomato and onion with a small amount of marinade and spread over the base of your pan. Place your chicken pieces onto the base of the pan, coat the potato wedges with a little more marinade and layer them around the chicken. Layer the sliced onion and sliced tomato over the chicken and potato and fill any gaps with the olives. Combine the remaining marinade with the coriander and water and pour over the top. Decorate with the preserved lemon. Cover your dish with the lid and cook on the stove top over a very low heat for 45 minutes. Don't stir or lift the lid during cooking. Serve from the tagine with couscous or rice.

Serves 4.

shepherd's pie

STEVE VALLIE
Head/Neck/Throat Cancer

My strongest memory of Dad was of him sipping a cup of tea. Sipping but never finishing it – he must have made at least ten a day but would have only drunk a total of two! As his cancer progressed he ate less and less but I know he preferred 'comfort food'. Shepherd's pie, mash potatoes and roast dinners with gravy. Anything that was easy to eat. Also, he loved a particular coffee shop in Hornsby and always ordered an iced coffee, although again he never drank it. I know it was a routine for him that gave him comfort and made him, for a short time, feel 'normal' and like everyone else. Tea and iced coffee are my strongest food memories. We miss him terribly – love you, Dad.

1 tablespoon olive oil
1 medium onion, finely chopped
500 g cooked lamb mince
2 carrots, finely diced
¼ butternut pumpkin, finely chopped
pinch mixed herbs
1 teaspoon cumin
1 tablespoon fresh parsley, chopped
2 tablespoons tomato purée
2 cups beef stock
salt and pepper, to taste
4 potatoes, peeled and chopped
1 sweet potato, peeled and chopped
40 g butter
125 ml (½ cup) milk
melted butter, to brush

Preheat oven to 180°C. Heat oil in a large saucepan and add onions and cook until soft. Add mince, stirring to break-up any lumps, carrots and pumpkin and cook for about 10–15 minutes, or until the mince changes colour and the vegetables are slightly browned. Add mixed herbs, cumin and parsley. Stir tomato purée into beef stock and pour into the pan. Bring to the boil then simmer for 5 minutes, or until sauce thickens a little. Season with salt and pepper to taste. Meanwhile, for the mash, cook potato and sweet potato in a saucepan of boiling salted water until tender. Drain well and return to the pan. Add the butter and milk and, using a potato masher, mash until smooth. Season with salt and pepper to taste. Spoon lamb mixture into a medium size ovenproof baking dish. Top with mashed potato and use a fork to spread over the lamb mixture. Brush with butter. Bake for 20–25 minutes or until mashed potato is golden brown. Serve immediately.

Serves 4.

crumbed lamb's fry

MRS MARGOT GEORGINA MOULDS
Breast Cancer

I had three beers every day – late afternoon, around 6–7 pm. Then I'd be right for the night. Made me feel good and gave me a good appetite.

300 g lamb's liver
milk, for soaking
2 cups fresh breadcrumbs
2 eggs
salt and pepper, to taste
oil, for frying

Day 1. Place liver in a bowl and pour over milk – just enough to cover it. Refrigerate overnight.

Day 2. Drain. Remove skin and pat dry. Thinly slice the liver. Put breadcrumbs in a shallow dish, season with salt and pepper. Beat eggs in a bowl. Run the lamb's fry through the egg, then toss through the breadcrumbs and set aside on a plate. Cover and leave in the fridge for 3 hours. Heat oil in a frying pan. Place the crumbed lamb's fry in the oil and cook for 1½ minutes each side, or until the breadcrumbs are golden. Serve with a fresh salad.

Serves 2.

the original cornish pasty

SANDRA SPINKS FOR SIMONNE RENVOIZE
Breast Cancer

This recipe is in memory of my very dear friend, Simonne Renvoize. Simonne was born in Cornwall, in the UK, home of the original Cornish Pasty. She was very proud of her roots, and there were two important things in her life – surfing and cancer. Her involvement in surfing led her, for part of her life, to live in Sydney, where her husband was a writer for Tracks Surfing Magazine. *In 1990 she was diagnosed with breast cancer, and after a long, painful illness sadly passed away in 1995.*

Throughout her journey with the illness she campaigned tirelessly to support the Macmillan Appeal. This organisation was raising funds to build a specialist breast cancer centre at Treliske Hospital (now the Royal Cornwall Hospital), Truro, Cornwall, which in turn would give other women the opportunity to receive the best possible diagnosis and treatment available. Sadly she was too ill to attend the launch, and although she was very modest in her achievements, we were all very proud of her when they named a wing in the Mermaid Centre in her memory for her tremendous input.

So, Simonne, this is for you!

for the pastry
525 g plain flour
pinch salt
245 g lard
cold water, to mix

To make the pastry, mix the dry ingredients in a bowl. Rub the lard into the flour with your fingertips until it resembles breadcrumbs. Add water a little at a time until the dough binds together. Work as quickly as possible to stop the dough from becoming warm. If the dough is dry and won't hold together, add more water, a teaspoon at a time. Gather the dough into a ball and press firmly. Cover with plastic wrap and refrigerate while you make the filling.

for the filling

1 medium turnip (swede)

1 large onion

1 large potato

450 g skirt or chuck steak,
diced into small pieces

salt and pepper

2–3 knobs of butter

beaten egg, to glaze

To make the filling, preheat oven to 180°C. Prepare all the vegetables by peeling and chopping into small even-sized pieces. Roll out the pastry. Cut large circles in the pastry and place on a lightly floured workbench. Assemble the ingredients on each circle, starting with the meat, then layering the turnip, onion and potato. Season with salt and pepper and top with a knob of butter. Brush the rim of the pastry with the egg, fold over the ingredients and 'crimp' the edges with a fork to seal. Make a hole in the top to release the steam while cooking. Place pasties on a well-greased baking tray. Brush with the egg and bake in the oven for 40–45 minutes or until golden brown.

Enjoy the aroma while they are cooking.

tip

I commenced chemo on 14 February, the day when most romantics get flowers. I lived a long way from my treatment centre (a six-hour drive) and found that wheatgrass shots from a city Boost Juice franchise gave me energy and assisted with my nausea. The colour would be enough to turn most people off, but it did help me, together with a frozen fruit smoothie with immune boosters.

I still seek out wheatgrass whenever I am near a franchise, but you can also buy it in powder form from health foods stores and mix it up yourself.

Pauline Venn – no diagnosis given

daube wagyu beef cheeks with baby carrots, leeks, button mushrooms, paris mash and a red wine reduction

GUILLAUME BRAHIMI

One day in November 2006, Chris sent me a text saying he was seriously ill with a brain tumour. I remember staring at the phone in utter disbelief. With his typical vigour, Chris didn't sit around for long. The way he dealt with his diagnosis was what sets him apart from most of us mere mortals. He used his own experience as a way to lobby the Government harder, so that he could realise his dream of building and opening the Sydney Cancer Centre. I remember dropping by lots of food for Chris, Gail, Adam, Juliette and James. I think in times of stress it's good to sit down and break bread together with your family and friends. They loved the beef daube, which feels quite nourishing for the soul. When Chris felt up to it, Gail said he would rummage around in the cellar for a great bottle of Burgundy to go with it.

50 ml olive oil

4 portions wagyu beef cheeks (250 g each), trimmed

2 litres red wine

1 carrot, peeled and cut into 2 cm cubes

1 onion, peeled and cut into 2 cm cubes

1 stick celery, cut into 2 cm cubes

4 cloves garlic

5 sprigs thyme

30 g speck, diced

1 teaspoon cracked white pepper

30 ml brandy

zest of 1 orange

DAY 1

Heat olive oil in a frying pan over high heat.

Seal the beef cheeks on both sides until golden brown (approximately 1 minute each side). Remove and set aside.

In a pot over high heat, bring wine to the boil and flame it. (Light the wine and let it burn until the flame goes out.) Set aside in a container to cool.

Place beef, carrot, onion, celery, garlic, thyme, speck and pepper into the wine, cover and refrigerate overnight.

DAY 2

Preheat oven to 180°C.

Bring the beef cheeks, vegetables and wine to the boil. Place in an ovenproof dish, cover and cook in the oven for 4 hours. Remove and allow to cool. Refrigerate overnight.

DAY 3

Preheat oven to 180°C.

Bring the beef cheeks, vegetables and wine to the boil. Add the brandy and orange zest. Place in an ovenproof dish, cover and cook in the oven for 2 hours. Remove from oven and set aside.

Using half the cooking liquid and butter, cook the carrots, leeks, mushrooms and speck in a pot over medium heat until softened.

Just before serving, cook croutons in a frying pan with the clarified butter, garlic and parsley.

To serve, place a scoop of mash (see below) into each bowl, top with beef cheeks, place vegetables and speck around the cheek and top with 2 tablespoons of sauce over the cheek. Sprinkle with croutons and chives and serve.

40 g butter
8 baby carrots, peeled
8 baby leeks, white part only, root and green removed, cut into 5 cm batons
100 g button mushrooms, stalks removed
100 g speck, diced
60 g croutons
25 g clarified butter
1 small garlic clove, finely chopped
½ teaspoon parsley, chopped
½ bunch chives, finely chopped

10 desiree potatoes (600 g)
100 g butter
300 ml milk
salt

PARIS MASH METHOD

Place the potatoes whole (with skin still on) into a pot of cold water. Bring to the boil and add salt. Cook until soft. Peel while still hot. Pass through tamis.

Heat milk in a saucepan until simmering. While the milk is heating, return the mashed potatoes to their pot and stir over medium heat for about 3–5 minutes to remove excess water (this will also add air to the potatoes to make them more light and fluffy). Add milk and stir in the butter. Mix until combined.

george's vegetable lasagne

GEORGE
No diagnosis given

olive oil
2–3 cloves garlic, crushed
½ leek, finely sliced
2 zucchini, sliced
3 sticks celery, sliced
5–6 mushrooms, sliced
1 large carrot, finely sliced
2 x 400 g tins tomatoes with roasted capsicums
1 jar cherry tomato and basil sauce
handful fresh basil, chopped
1 tablespoon brown sugar
½ cup red wine, optional
salt and pepper, to taste
1 packet fresh lasagne sheets

cheese sauce
1 heaped tablespoon cornflour
½ cup milk
500 ml milk
½ cup cheddar cheese, grated
salt and pepper, to taste

Preheat oven to 160°C. Heat oil in a saucepan and sauté the vegetables until just tender. Add the tinned tomatoes and jar of tomato sauce. Add basil, sugar and wine and simmer for 20 minutes. Season with salt and pepper to taste. For the cheese sauce, combine the cornflour and ½ cup milk and mix well. Heat 500 ml milk in a saucepan and when warm add the cornflour mixture and stir constantly until it thickens. Stir in cheese and season with salt and pepper. Remove from heat.

To make the lasagne: spoon a little of the tomato sauce (without getting any vegetables if you can) in the bottom of a lasagne dish – just enough to wet it. Then start layering: first a lasagne sheet, then a layer of tomato mixture and then some cheese sauce. Repeat the layering until you finish with a lasagne sheet on top. Top with a thin layer of tomato sauce and finish with the cheese sauce on top. Cook in the oven for 30 minutes and serve. Tastes even better the next day.

Serves 2.

simple fettuccine

STEVEN BALLAS
No diagnosis given

salt
1 packet of fettuccine
olive oil
7 slices pancetta, diced, or
prosciutto, finely chopped
1 red capsicum, diced
3 cloves garlic, crushed
1 teaspoon chilli paste, optional
handful of parsley, finely
chopped
1 punnet cherry tomatoes,
quartered
handful of pine nuts
salt and pepper, to taste
pecorino cheese, optional

Bring a large pot of water to the boil. Add salt and the fettuccine, and return to a rolling boil. Cook for 10 minutes or until the pasta is al dente. While the pasta is cooking, in a deep pan, heat the olive oil then add the pancetta or prosciutto and cook for 2 minutes, stirring. Add the capsicum, garlic and chilli paste. Keep stirring and rotating the ingredients and cook for 2 minutes. Add the parsley, quartered tomatoes and pine nuts. Cook for approximately 5 minutes or until the tomatoes become just soft. Drain the fettuccine and place into a large serving platter. Pour all of the cooked ingredients on top and stir in well. Add salt and pepper to taste. Top with grated pecorino cheese.

Serves 4–6.

tip

Seasick bands on wrists before getting up in the morning, and slivers of ginger steeped in boiling water helps with nausea. Use a soft toothbrush if mouth is sore and a little certified Manuka honey on mouth ulcers helps soothe the pain.

Grace Dureau – Breast Cancer

macaroni cheese

MAGGIE BEER

My mother often made this rich and luscious dish when we had relatives coming to dinner. Now, when I think about the small oven she had to work with, it makes sense that she chose to bake a dish that took maximum advantage of the limited space available. Mum never wrote down a recipe in her life, so I only have the memory of what she did to go by. I remember that, even when I was a child, she'd use the sharpest possible cheese she could find (in those days it was a New Zealand Epicure cheese). I have contributed my own touch, adding roasted pumpkin and Persian feta. It definitely needs to be served with a bitter leaf salad alongside; my stock in trade one is made with radicchio, rocket and witlof, dressed with a good vinaigrette.

1.2 kg jap or queensland blue pumpkin, peeled, seeded and cut into small chunks
4 stalks rosemary, leaves picked and chopped
sea salt
extra virgin olive oil, for cooking
¼ cup verjuice
2 litres milk
2 fresh bay leaves
160 g unsalted butter, chopped
160 g plain flour
1 tablespoon freshly grated or ground nutmeg
250 g parmigiano reggiano, grated
400 g large macaroni
150 g persian goat's feta, crumbled
250 g cheddar, grated

Preheat fan-forced oven to 220°C.

Line a baking tray with baking paper, then add pumpkin and rosemary, season generously with salt and drizzle with olive oil. Roast for 30 minutes or until pumpkin is tender and starting to brown. Take tray out of oven, then drizzle verjuice over pumpkin. Return tray to oven and cook until verjuice has evaporated.

Meanwhile, heat milk with bay leaves in a saucepan over high heat until almost boiling, then remove from heat and leave to infuse for 10 minutes. Remove and discard bay leaves and keep milk hot.

Melt butter in a saucepan over medium heat until nut-brown. Add flour and cook until flour and butter come together, stirring for several minutes. Remove from heat and slowly pour in hot milk, using a whisk to incorporate and prevent any lumps from forming. Return to the heat and stir with a wooden spoon for another 10 minutes, or until the sauce is shiny and coats the back of the spoon. Add nutmeg and grated Parmigiano Reggiano, stirring continuously until the cheese has melted.

Taste the sauce to see if any salt is necessary; take care to only season with salt after you've added the grated Parmigiano Reggiano as it can be salty enough. Cover the surface of sauce closely with plastic film to stop a skin from forming and set aside until needed.

Cook macaroni in a large saucepan of boiling salted water until al dente, then drain and place in a large mixing bowl. Add the cheese sauce to the macaroni and mix through well, then add the pumpkin and toss through gently. Gently stir in the crumbled feta. Transfer the macaroni mixture to a large 2.5 litre baking dish (mine is a 40 x 30 x 5 cm), top with grated cheddar and bake for 10–20 minutes, or until brown. Serve immediately.

meatless spaghetti bolognese

TIM

No diagnosis given

I was told to eat less meat but I love spaghetti bolognese – here is my meatless version I ate while undergoing chemo.

1 tablespoon olive oil

2 cloves garlic, crushed

1 onion, chopped

200 g mushrooms, sliced

1 zucchini, sliced

2 x 400 g tin chopped tomatoes with basil

plenty of fresh basil leaves, or dried basil

400 g tin organic brown lentils

splash of red wine, optional

1 teaspoon sugar

spaghetti, to serve

salt and pepper, to taste

Heat oil in a heavy-based pan. Add all vegetables and cook for 5 minutes, stirring. Add tins of tomatoes and basil and cook for a few minutes longer. Add lentils, wine and sugar and stir through. Season with salt and pepper to taste. Simmer, stirring occasionally, for 15–20 minutes. Meanwhile, cook spaghetti in salted boiling water until al dente. Drain. Add the sauce to the pasta and serve.

The sauce can be frozen in portions.

Serves 2–4.

tortellini with mushroom sauce

NO NAME GIVEN

Breast Cancer

250 g tortellini

1 tablespoon olive oil

225 g mushrooms, sliced

bunch shallots, trimmed and sliced

pinch cinnamon powder

100 g hummus

2 tablespoons milk or cream

salt and pepper, to taste

Cook the tortellini in a large pot of salted boiling water until al dente. While the tortellini is cooking, heat the oil in a pan. Add the mushrooms, shallots and cinnamon and cook for 2–3 minutes. Add the hummus and milk or cream, cover and simmer for 5–10 minutes. When the tortellini is cooked, drain the pasta and stir in the mushroom sauce. Season to taste, adding more cinnamon if desired.

Serves 2.

tip

My carers maintained a food chart with time/food eaten each day to monitor food and liquid intake. Multivitamins (Centrium), Iron, Vitamin B Complex, Vitamin C powder. Ginger ale, ginger tea or juices with fresh ginger aids with nausea. Salty foods help with taste.

Ruth Milonas – Lung Cancer

penne all'arrabbiata

ROSARIA MANTARRO
Lung Cancer and Breast Cancer

3 tablespoons olive oil

2 cloves garlic, chopped

1–2 dried chilli peppers, chopped or small red chillies, seeded and chopped

1 x 400 g tin tomatoes or bottle of passata

salt and pepper, to taste

375 g penne pasta

2 tablespoons parsley, chopped

75 g fresh parmesan, grated

Heat oil in a large saucepan. Quickly fry the garlic and chilli (for about 1 minute). Add tomatoes or passata and cook for 15 minutes. Season with salt and pepper to taste. Meanwhile, cook pasta in salted boiling water until al dente. Drain. Add the pasta and parsley to sauce and stir through until mixed well. Serve with parmesan.

Serves 4.

quick macaroni cheese

CHARLES HAGENBACH
Testicular Cancer

250 g macaroni pasta

300 g strong cheddar cheese, grated

½ cup milk or cream

salt and pepper, to taste

10–12 broccoli florets

Place pasta in a large pot, cover with water and bring to the boil then reduce heat to simmer, until all the water is gone and the pasta is soft, being careful not to burn the pasta dry. Stir in the cheese and milk. Season with salt and pepper, then stir in broccoli. Preheat oven to 170°C. Pour pasta mixture into an ovenproof dish and bake for 30 minutes or until golden brown.

Serves 2.

greek pasta

ANTHONY GEORGIOU
Synovial Sarcoma/Lung Cancer

200 g hilopites (Greek handmade pasta)
½ cup plain Greek style yoghurt
1 tablespoon dried mint
salt and pepper, to taste

In a large heavy-based pot bring salted water to a rapid boil and add hilopites. Boil pasta until al dente and drain. Transfer to serving bowl and add yoghurt and mint, mix well and serve.

Variation: crumbled feta cheese and olive oil stirred through your favourite pasta.

Tip: for nausea, try plain boiled pasta stirred through with fried zucchini, lemon and salt.

Serves 2.

puttanesca sauce

SUSAN BURNET
Breast Cancer

2 tablespoons olive oil
3 cloves garlic, crushed
2 tablespoons fresh parsley, chopped
2 x 400 g tins crushed tomatoes
1 tablespoon capers
3 anchovy fillets, chopped
¼ cup black olives, chopped
black pepper, to taste

Heat oil in a pan and sauté garlic and parsley for about 1 minute.
Add tomato, bring to the boil then simmer covered for 5 minutes.
Add capers, anchovies and olives and simmer for a further 5 minutes.
Season with black pepper. Serve with your favourite pasta.

Makes 1 litre.

baked chicken and pumpkin risotto

CATHY BROWNE
Breast Cancer

I found this recipe invaluable during my chemo, as it takes very little preparation, and there aren't many cooking smells except when you fry the chicken – but you could also bake or poach it, or cook the chicken any way you like. I found it filling but not bloating, great tasting but not overpowering.

2 cups arborio or
other risotto rice
5 cups chicken stock
700 g pumpkin,
peeled and diced
3 chicken breast fillets
olive oil
½ cup pecorino, grated
cracked black pepper
2 tablespoons parsley, chopped

Preheat oven to 190°C. Place rice, stock and pumpkin in large ovenproof dish and cover tightly. Bake for 30 minutes or until the rice is soft. Meanwhile, in a heavy-based pan, cook chicken in olive oil, until cooked through. Allow to cool slightly, and then chop. Remove risotto from the oven, and stir in chicken, pecorino, pepper and parsley continuously, until risotto is creamy. Serve immediately.

Variation: use chicken strips instead of chicken breasts, so less cooking and chopping. Use sweet potato in place of the pumpkin. Or to add some greens, throw some peas in the rice towards the end of the cooking.

Serves 4.

sweet treats

rice pudding

baked custard

lemon tart

banana cake

the very best boiled fruit cake

roast peach with honey ricotta and pistachios

norm's peanut biscuits

hot chocolate au naturale

chickpea and chocolate chip cookies

strawberry mousse ice-cream

lily pilly granita, raspberries and sheep's milk ice-cream

other dessert suggestions

rice pudding

NO NAME GIVEN

Lung Cancer

I ate rice pudding all the time. Not only was it delicious, it was easy to digest.

1 tin carnation milk

1 litre milk

2 tablespoons brown sugar

2 tablespoons golden syrup

2 cups pudding rice

Preheat oven to 160°C. Put all the ingredients except the rice in a large saucepan and stir. Rinse the rice and add to the milk mixture. Bring to the boil then reduce heat to a gentle simmer and cook for 10 minutes, stirring occasionally so the rice doesn't catch on the base of the pan. Pour the mixture into a 3 litre pie dish and bake in the oven for 1–1½ hours, allowing the pudding to cook slowly and adding more milk if necessary. When the rice is cooked, remove from the oven and cool slightly before serving. Also great served with ice-cream.

Serves 4.

baked custard

ANNETTE McINERNEY

Ovarian Cancer

I like 'comfort' food like baked custard.

2 cups milk

2 eggs

pinch salt

2 tablespoons caster sugar

2 tablespoons nutmeg or cinnamon

Preheat oven to 160°C. Beat all ingredients together. Pour into four custard cups and sprinkle with more nutmeg or cinnamon. Place custard cups into a deep tray, then slowly pour hot water into the tray until it is almost to the top of the cup. Bake for 40–55 minutes or until set when tested with a knife. Allow to cool and serve warm or cover with plastic wrap and refrigerate until ready to serve.

Serves 4.

lemon tart

GUILLAUME BRAHIMI

Chris's favourite dessert was without a doubt this Lemon Tart. I think it made him feel so good, despite feeling anything but during his period of intensive chemotherapy. At one stage Chris even volunteered that he thought the Lemon Tart had medicinal qualities, as every time he had it, shortly after he would receive positive brain scan results. Chris never lost his sense of humour. He was quite honestly the best and kindest man I've ever met and I look forward to sharing some Lemon Tarts up high in the skies with him one day.

sweet pastry
300 g cold unsalted butter, diced
190 g icing sugar
65 g almond meal
2 eggs
500 g baker's flour
pinch salt
1 vanilla bean, split and seeds scraped

lemon curd
9 eggs
540 g sugar
10 lemons, juice and freshly grated zest
700 g cold unsalted butter, diced
3 sheets gelatine, softened in cold water and squeezed to remove excess liquid

Preheat oven to 180°C. Grease the bottom and sides of a 20 cm tart tin (with a removable base) and sprinkle with flour.

For the sweet pastry, combine the butter, icing sugar and almond meal in a large bowl and bind together. Add the eggs one at a time, and mix well. Sift in the flour, then add the salt and vanilla seeds, and mix well until combined. Wrap in plastic film and chill in the fridge for 20 minutes.

Roll out the pastry and place it in the prepared tart tin. Rest for 1 hour at room temperature, to prevent the pastry from shrinking.

Fill the pastry with rice or baking weights and blind bake for 15 minutes. Remove the rice and bake for a further 5 minutes or until the pastry is golden brown. Allow to cool completely.

Meanwhile, for the lemon curd, whisk the eggs and sugar in a heatproof bowl until light in colour, then add the lemon zest and juice. Place the bowl over a saucepan of gently boiling water (making sure the bottom of the bowl does not touch the water), and stir continuously until the mixture thickens. Do not allow it to boil.

Place the butter in a separate large bowl. Strain in the egg and lemon mixture, and mix with a stick blender until well combined. Add the gelatine, stir to combine.

Pour the lemon curd into the cooled tart shell and leave to set in the fridge for 6 hours. Cut into slices and serve.

banana cake

CORALIE BACKMAN
Breast Cancer

Be with people who have a calming influence in your life and make your life as stress-free as possible – even if it may be that you make enormous changes. Also try to eat lots.

125 g butter or good quality vegetable margarine

1 cup brown or raw sugar (or honey to taste)

1½ cups self-raising flour (wholemeal preferred)

2 eggs

1 teaspoon bicarbonate of soda

2 tablespoons milk or soy milk

2 teaspoons vanilla essence

3 medium-sized ripe bananas, mashed

Preheat oven to 190°C. Lightly grease and line a 23 cm round cake tin. In a mixer, on low speed, cream butter and sugar for 3–4 minutes. Slowly add all other ingredients and lightly mix until combined. Spoon batter into your cake tin. Bake for 40–45 minutes, or until an inserted knife comes out clean. Leave cake to cool in tin for approximately 10 minutes then turn out onto a rack. When cake is cool, ice or dust with icing sugar.

Variation: add chopped walnuts and/or dates, or a little cinnamon/mixed spice to the batter.

tip

Be positive from Day One, despite diagnosis, and keep sense of humour.

Stewart Aitken – Throat Cancer

the very best boiled fruit cake

NO NAME
Breast Cancer

1 kg fruit mix (australian)
250 g butter (not margarine)
1 cup brown sugar, firmly packed
½ cup brandy or whisky or sherry
½ cup water
5 eggs, lightly beaten
1 tablespoon treacle or golden syrup or honey
2 teaspoons grated orange rind
1 teaspoon grated lemon rind
1¾ cups plain flour
⅓ cup self-raising flour
½ teaspoon bicarbonate of soda

Combine fruit, butter, sugar, brandy and water in a large saucepan. Stir over medium heat to dissolve sugar, bring to the boil and simmer, covered, for 10 minutes. Allow to cool to room temperature (or leave out overnight). Grease a deep 23 cm round or 19 cm square cake tin, and line base and sides with baking paper – leaving enough for paper to come up above the sides of the tin. Preheat oven to 150°C. In a large mixing bowl stir eggs, treacle and orange and lemon rind into the fruit mix, then stir sifted flours and bicarbonate of soda into the mix. Spread evenly into the prepared cake tin and decorate with almonds and cherries if desired. Bake for 1½–2 hours – or until a skewer comes out clean when tested. Cover and cool in the tin.

roast peach with honey ricotta and pistachios

SERGE DANSEREAU

There is nothing more glorious than beautiful ripe peaches. When the peaches are perfect and you need a bit of a change from eating them fresh, just roast them quickly with a touch of butter and sugar. Serve them as the recipe suggests for breakfast or with any cake, biscuit or ice-cream for dessert.

3 tablespoons pistachios, roughly chopped
12 whole ripe peaches
½ cup (100 g) butter at room temperature
½ cup (100 g) brown sugar
1½ cups (200 g) soft ricotta
2 tablespoons honey

Preheat oven to 180°C.

Place the pistachios on an oven tray and put them in the oven at the same time as the peaches to toast and crisp them slightly. Remove when the peaches are ready.

Cut the peaches in half and remove the stone. Put them in a baking tray, cut face down. On top of each peach add a small amount of butter and top with some brown sugar and then place in the oven. After 5 minutes test to see if the skin is able to be removed. If the peaches are not quite ready, cook for another 2 minutes; this will depend on the ripeness of your peach. The idea is to barely cook them so the skin comes off but not to fully roast them. Take the peaches out of the oven, remove the skin and then cool.

Put the ricotta in a bowl of a mixer and beat at a low speed to soften. Add two-thirds of the pistachios and the honey and mix by hand for 1 minute.

To serve, put some of the ricotta mixture in a small bowl, top with the peach halves and a sprinkle of toasted pistachios. Drizzle with a little spoonful of roasting butter if you have this from the peach roasting tray.

norm's peanut biscuits

NORM

No diagnosis given

125 g softened butter
¾ cup brown sugar
1 egg
1 ½ cups self-raising flour
pinch salt
1 teaspoon baking powder
2 tablespoons chocolate powder
1 cup chopped peanuts
(granulated nuts are okay)

Preheat oven to 180°C. In a large mixing bowl cream butter and sugar. Add egg, flour, salt, baking powder, chocolate powder and peanuts. The dough will be quite stiff, mix well. Roll into about 24–26 balls and place on a lined baking tray. Flatten the balls a little with a fork. Bake for 15 minutes. Yum!

Good to take to hospital visits for nibbles.

Makes 2 dozen.

hot chocolate au naturale

30 g cocoa powder nibs
¼ teaspoon cloves
1 tablespoon cinnamon
½ teaspoon nutmeg
1 cup/mug milk

Pulse the cocoa nibs in a coffee grinder 3–4 times until the nibs are coarsely chopped. Then place all dry ingredients in a blender and blend until smooth. Pour milk in a pan, add cocoa mixture and heat gently, stirring the cocoa mixture through, before serving.

Makes 1 cup.

chickpea and chocolate chip cookies

BARRY AND AUDREY MYRDEN

No diagnosis given

1 can chickpeas (ideally organic), drained
⅓ cup brown sugar
½ cup olive oil
½ cup plain yoghurt
1 teaspoon vanilla
pinch of cinnamon
½ cup dark chocolate chips
2 cups wholemeal self-raising flour
½ cup oats

Preheat oven to 180°C. Mash chickpeas with a fork and set aside. In a large bowl, beat sugar and oil. Add yoghurt, vanilla and cinnamon and beat until smooth. Add mashed chickpeas and chocolate chips and combine. Add flour and oats and mix well. Pick up rounded tablespoon-sized pieces of dough and roll into balls. Fork press onto a lightly greased non-stick baking tray. Bake for 11–13 minutes (don't over bake). Allow to cool. Keep in airtight container for 3 days (or 3 months in the freezer).

Options: as these little gems are made with olive oil and freeze up nicely, they can be served and eaten frozen.

Makes 3 dozen.

strawberry mousse ice-cream

GRACE DUREAU
Breast Cancer

This is so very easy and tastes delicious. It has such a cleansing taste on a hot day.

2 punnets strawberries, stems hulled

juice of 2 lemons

275 g caster sugar

1 x 300 ml carton cream

Place strawberries, lemon juice and sugar in a blender or food processor. Blend and allow to stand/soak for 10 minutes until sugar is dissolved. Meanwhile, beat cream until soft peaks are formed, then fold in the strawberry mix. Pour into a container and put in the freezer. It's that easy! To serve, remove from freezer 15 minutes before serving. The strawberry/sugar quantities are best tested by tasting – it needs to have a 'bite'. Can be served with little meringues.

Variation: 1 tin crushed pineapple, 2 tablespoons desiccated coconut, 2 tablespoons lemon juice, 1 tablespoon Malibu (optional), 150 g caster sugar, 1 x 300 ml carton cream. Method as above.

Serves 4.

tip

Fresh lemon and ginger tea, with a little honey to sweeten, for sickness. Chop up a whole lemon, including the peel.

Timothy Stinton – Lymphoma

lily pilly granita, raspberries and sheep's milk ice-cream

PETER GILMORE

sheep's milk ice-cream
500 ml fresh sheep's milk
5 egg yolks
250 g caster sugar
2 punnets fresh raspberries

lily pilly granita
1 litre water
300 g sugar
2 vanilla beans
400 g fresh or frozen lily pillies

For the sheep's milk ice-cream, warm sheep's milk in a small saucepan until it reaches 90 degrees. Whisk egg yolks and sugar in a bowl. Pour on hot sheep's milk while whisking. Return to a saucepan and stir constantly until slightly thickened. Place mixture in an upright blender.

Blend on high for 2 minutes. Pass the mixture through a fine sieve. Refrigerate overnight and churn mixture in ice-cream machine just 3 hours before serving.

For the Lily Pilly Granita, in a small saucepan add water and sugar with two scraped vanilla beans. Bring to the boil. Pour onto deseeded lily pillies. Place back on heat and simmer for 2 minutes. Take off heat and allow to cool slightly.

Once mixture is cool enough to handle, wearing a pair of gloves squeeze the lily pilly fruit into the syrup with your hands. Allow the syrup and fruit to infuse for 2 hours, then strain through a fine sieve, discard the solids and place syrup in a bowl and freeze. Allow to freeze for 24 hours.

To finish and serve

Take 8 serving glasses and, using a fork, shave the lily pilly granita and fill each glass with a couple of spoonfuls of granita. Scatter 10–15 fresh raspberries through the granita. Top with one more spoonful of granita. Place a quenelled spoonful of freshly churned sheep's milk ice-cream on top of each granita.

Serve immediately.

other dessert suggestions

LEE McKERRACHER
Breast Cancer

When I was undergoing chemo I really didn't want to be bothered about food, but I knew I had to eat and at least try to keep my fluids up. Here are a few easy things I did.

fruity pops

Cut some strawberries (or whatever berries you have) and pop them into ice block moulds. Fill the moulds with orange juice and freeze. You can also use individual ice cube trays and have small portions to suck when you need some fluid.

banana bliss

Peel a banana, wrap it in foil and pop it in the freezer. Once frozen you have a great icy treat that is sugar free and not too much effort to eat. If you feel inclined, you can dip the banana in melted chocolate prior to sticking it in the freezer (wrapped in foil of course).

pineapple indulgence

Cut a pineapple into thick, long strips that you can insert a skewer into. Throw them on a BBQ and caramelize on each side. Dip into melted chocolate, desiccated coconut and enjoy. For an adult version, pop some Cointreau or Grand Marnier into the chocolate. This last one was for when I was starting to feel much better!

I found ginger beer and boiled lollies wonderful for taste when taking chemo orally. Magnesium Forte for cramps, and meditation.

KEITH KING
Shoulder Cancer

McDonald's strawberry thick shakes helped with loss of taste. Berocca for vitamins. For anyone with Type 2 diabetes, chemo affects your sugar levels so it's important to go to a diabetic clinic and to drink lots of water every day.

ALAN DIAMOND
Lung Cancer

Take a tape recorder with you when you go to the doctors as you don't always take in all they are saying, especially when you've been told what you have. It's often not so bad when you listen the second time!

CHARLES HAGENBACH
Testicular Cancer

For dry mouth – water with a squeeze of lemon juice. And acupuncture on wrist for chemo nausea.

ANTHONY GEORGIOU
Lung Cancer

Support from friends and family helped me get through the chemotherapy. My very dear friends drew up a roster and accompanied me on each visit. We would make it special by going somewhere for lunch or coffee after the session.

I found it important to let out any negative feelings – not to bottle them up, this is where my support team was invaluable. They were always happy to listen. Try to keep busy with work/hobbies/sport. Plan something special to look forward to at the end of treatment. Maybe a holiday or something you have always thought about but somehow never seemed to have the time – reward and pamper yourself!

I found that while on chemo I needed strong tasting foods and drinks to help combat the metallic taste in my mouth – raw almonds helped. Freshly squeezed carrot, celery, beetroot and ginger juice for tiredness, and herbal 'sleepy time' tea for sleep.

CHRISTINE BELL
Breast Cancer

Meditation helped with sleep, as well as a few drops of lavender
oil on a handkerchief next to my pillow.

LAURETTE FOMIATTI
Colon Cancer

Herbal teas (particularly prior to
eating) helped with taste.

JOE LECHOWSKI
Liver Cancer

Magnesium tablets help with my 'funny legs'.

LINDA REID
Cervical Cancer

Be proactive with your medication: take whatever you're told to take, whenever you're told to take it —
don't wait for side effects to appear before you decide to deal with them. Give your medical oncologist
and infusion pharmacist feedback as to how your medication affects you — they can often make you more
comfortable with a different dosage or tablet.

Make sure you sleep well at night. Discuss this with your oncologist or pharmacist and get tablets if you need
them, just for this time. Drink as much reasonable quality fluid as you can. Get as much exercise as you can. If
you can only manage laps of the kitchen, then do that as often as you can.

Take the risk of lymphoedema seriously, just for now, by doing your exercises and massage regularly. They're
really important for the rehabilitation of your 'surgery' arm, too.

Surround yourself with positive, supportive, kind and knowledgeable people. If people whom you've
considered good friends, or family members, aren't this way, then limit your exposure to them. Group emails
can be very useful to keep people 'in the loop' with your news, and cut down the number of enquiries you
have to field, as sometimes you may be too tired even to answer the phone. Group emails also help address
the issue of friends and family who want news of you, but don't know whether they'll disturb you if they
contact you, or even whether they should contact you at all.

Take whatever help is offered that you want to take.

Be kind to yourself.

Remember, there are no 'right and wrong' rules as to what will help you through chemo.
Whatever works for you, is right!

CATHY BROWNE
SAN Breast Cancer Exercise & Support Group

Please consider making a tax-deductible donation to Chris O'Brien Lifehouse. Your gift will help fund an array of patient services at Lifehouse. For more information, or to make a secure online donation,

*visit our website **mylifehouse.org.au***

You can also donate via credit card, cheque or money order by completing your details below and returning to:

CHRIS O'BRIEN LIFEHOUSE
MAIL: PO BOX M5, MISSENDEN ROAD NSW 2050
EMAIL: FUNDRAISING@LH.ORG.AU
FAX: (02) 8514 0901
PHONE: 1300 852 500

Title:_____ First name:_____Surname:_____

Organisation (if applicable): _____

Address: _____

_____

Suburb: _____Postcode: _____

Telephone (Day):_____ (Mobile): _____

Email: _____

I wish to donate $_____

Credit Card Payment

Card Type: □ Amex   □ Mastercard   □ Visa

Card Number: _____ Expiry Date:___/____

Cardholder's Name: _____

Cardholder's Signature: _____

Please make cheques/money orders payable to Chris O'Brien Lifehouse

Thank you for your kind donation. Your tax–deductible receipt will be sent shortly.
ABN: 70 388 962 804